# The Spies and Detectives Cut and Colour Book

Kingfisher Books

Kingfisher Books, Grisewood & Dempsey Ltd,
Elsley House, 24–30 Great Titchfield Street,
London W1P 7AD

First published in 1989 by Kingfisher Books

Copyright © Grisewood & Dempsey Ltd 1989

All rights reserved. No part of this publication may be reproduced, stored in a retrieval system or transmitted by any means, electronic, mechanical, photocopying or otherwise, without the prior permission of the publisher.

BRITISH LIBRARY CATALOGUING IN PUBLICATION DATA
Robins, Deri
  Spies and detectives cut and colour book
  1. Espionage
  I. Title  II. Series
  327.1'2

ISBN 0-86272-404-X

Editor: Deri Robins
Designer: Ben White
Illustrated by: Jim Robins, Pete Chesterton, Peter Stephenson (*Jillian Burgess*) and David Bowyer (*Jillian Burgess*)

Photoset by Rowland Phototypesetting Ltd,
Bury St Edmunds, Suffolk
Printed and bound in Spain

Note: Many of the activities in this book use glue. Please use either children's glue or glue sticks. For building the model of Sherlock Holmes' study, double-sided sellotape can be used in place of glue.

# C.O.N.T.E.N.T.S

| | |
|---|---|
| **Setting up in Business** | 4 |
| **Detective Badges** | 6 |
| **A Peephole Newspaper** | 7 |
| **Shadowing Suspects** | 8 |
| **Fingerprint Kit** | 10 |
| **The Blue Carbuncle** (adapted from the story by Sir Arthur Conan Doyle) | 12 |
| **Make a Walkie-Talkie** | 20 |
| **Bank Raid** | 21 |
| **I-D Kit** | 23 |
| **The Pyramid Murders** | 28 |
| **Spyfile** | 30 |
| **Foolproof Disguises** | 32 |
| **A Spy in Your Wardrobe** | 34 |
| **Mirror Image** | 36 |
| **Spytracker** | 37 |
| **Keeping Secrets Really Safe** | 38 |
| **Clever Codes** | 40 |
| **Make a Code Wheel** | 42 |
| **The Lost Codebook** | 44 |
| **The Totally Secret Party** | 46 |
| **Answers** | 48 |

# Setting up in Business

So you want to be a detective?
If you really mean business, the first thing to do is to work up a really professional image. To begin with, you'll need an office – so make an official-looking sign to hang on your bedroom door. You could also cut out letters and stick them on the window (see below).

AN IDENTITY CARD – **MAKE YOUR OWN!**

AN **OFFICE** IN TOWN (YOUR BEDROOM WILL DO).

THE BEST PRIVATE EYES HAVE 1938 FORD CONVERTIBLES. SEE WHAT YOU CAN DO WITH YOUR **BIKE!**

A COAT WITH A **BIG COLLAR** – A REAL DETECTIVE **MUST!**

Collect all the unwanted junk mail that comes through the post, and cut out any official-looking headings you may find. Stick them onto plain paper and write your agency's name underneath. Perhaps you could persuade an adult to photocopy this for you? Or maybe you could borrow some official rubber stamps from someone's office, to print your stationery?

**KEEP YOUR EYES OPEN** FOR SPECIAL STAMPS LIKE THIS.

**QUITE A LOT OF JUNK MAIL** CONTAINS USEFUL-LOOKING BITS OF MATERIAL.

MAKE **BADGES** OUT OF CARD. STICK SAFETY PINS ON THE BACK WITH SELLOTAPE.

# Detective Badges

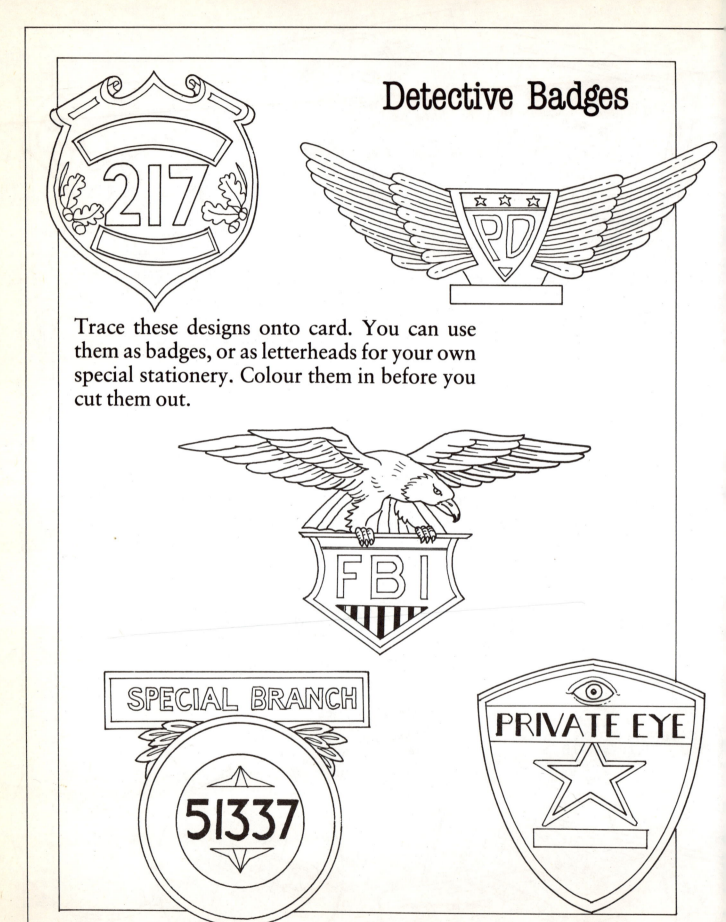

Trace these designs onto card. You can use them as badges, or as letterheads for your own special stationery. Colour them in before you cut them out.

# A Peephole Newspaper

If you are following a suspect who knows you by sight, this is a great way of staying out of view while keeping a close eye on the action!

*All you need are: A paper or a magazine; glue; scissors.*

Glue four or five sheets of your paper or magazine together. When it is dry, hold it up in front of you, and mark the spot where you want the peepholes to be. Cut small holes out carefully with nail scissors.

Cut holes for eyes

Glue sheets together

# Shadowing Suspects

A top detective has to be as secretive as a spy, as coolly logical as a scientist and as cunning as a master criminal. Added to this, he or she needs a number of special skills.

One of the most important skills is knowing how to follow a suspect without being spotted yourself. Here are some inside tips from the professionals!

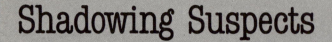

1. Try to blend into the background as much as possible by dressing in an ordinary way. (This is one occasion when the trenchcoat should be left behind.)

2. Learn to follow your suspect at a discreet distance. This detective is TOO CLOSE.

3. Stay close enough to make sure you don't lose the suspect. This detective is TOO FAR AWAY.

BEAT IT, SMALL-CHANGE!

GET YOURSELF SOME **WHEELS**!

4. Make sure you have some transport handy in case of a quick getaway!

5. Always carry a paper to hide behind. A peephole newspaper is best (see page 7). This will help you look a lot less suspicious if you have to lurk in the same place for a long period of time.

6. If you are watching a suspect's house, make sure that you are clued up about all the back entrances. This detective is in for a long night's wait.

# Fingerprint Kit

Every detective knows that no two person's fingerprints are alike. This is why they are one of the first things detectives look for at the scene of the crime. Here is how you can make a fingerprint kit.

*To put your family's fingerprints on record, you will need: An ink pad (or some cotton wool soaked in ink or dark poster paint); some white card.*

Practise taking your own prints first. Press your right thumb lightly onto the pad and roll from side to side. Now press lightly onto the card, rolling the thumb again. Repeat with each finger of that hand. Write your name clearly at the top of the card, and label each finger correctly. Repeat for the left hand. Now ask your family to do the same.

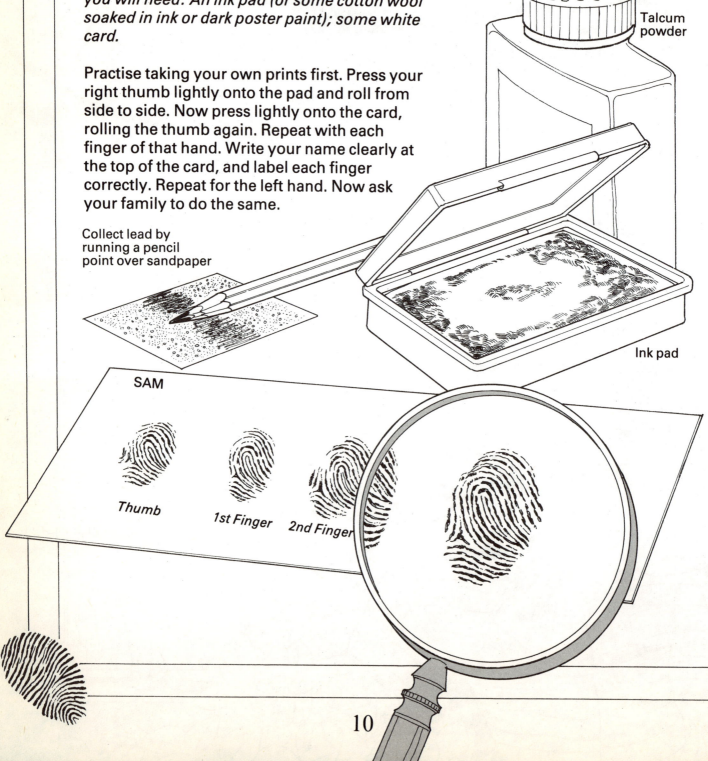

Collect lead by running a pencil point over sandpaper

Talcum powder

Ink pad

SAM

Thumb    1st Finger    2nd Finger

## TESTING FOR PRINTS

*To test for fingerprints, you will need: Talcum powder (for testing dark surfaces); some ground pencil lead or some cocoa (for light surfaces); a soft paintbrush; some clear sticky tape.*

Brush the powder very gently over any surface where you think a fingerprint might be. If a print appears, cut a piece of clear sticky tape and press it very firmly over the print. Lift it up carefully, and stick it onto some card – if you've used a dark powder to show up the print, stick onto white card, and the other way round.

Compare the new print with the ones in your Fingerprint File, and see if you can identify the owner of the guilty finger!

## FINGERPRINT TYPES

Look closely at the fingerprints. Do they have an arch, a loop or a whorl in the centre? The four shown below are the most common types of fingerprint.

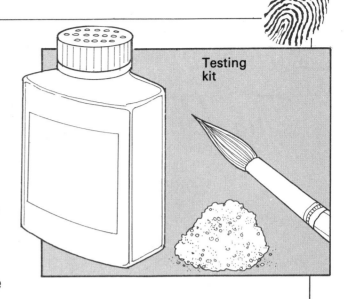
Testing kit

Brush gently until print appears

Stick tape firmly over print

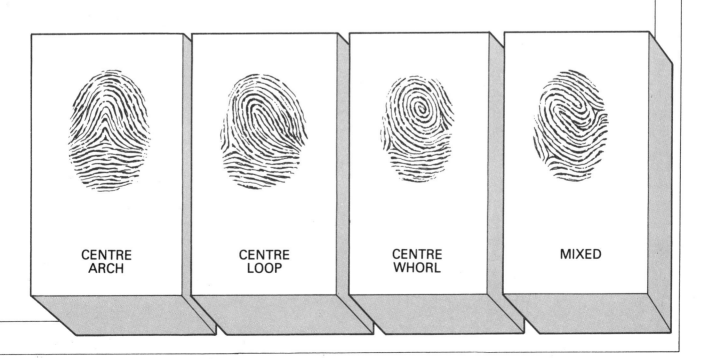
CENTRE ARCH  CENTRE LOOP  CENTRE WHORL  MIXED

## HOTEL COSMOPOLITAN JEWEL ROBBERY

John Horner, plumber, was arrested today for the theft of the valuable gem known as the blue carbuncle. The jewel was stolen from the Countess of Morca's rooms at the Hotel Cosmopolitan.

Horner was arrested on the evidence of James Ryder, an attendant at the hotel. On the day of the robbery, Ryder had shown Horner to the Countess' rooms to fix a leaking pipe. Ryder was then called away, and on his return found that the dresser had been forced open and an empty jewel case was lying on top. Horner was nowhere to be seen.

The police report that Horner resisted arrest, claiming that he was innocent. The case has been referred to the criminal court.

*THE QUESTION, WATSON, IS HOW THE JEWEL GOT FROM THE COUNTESS' JEWEL BOX TO THE GOOSE! I THINK IT'S TIME WE HAD A WORD WITH MR HENRY BAKER...*

AT THIS, THE GREAT DETECTIVE REACHED FOR A PENCIL AND A SLIP OF PAPER, AND WROTE OUT THE FOLLOWING ADVERTISEMENT:

"FOUND. ONE GOOSE AND ONE HAT. MR HENRY BAKER MAY COLLECT FROM 221B BAKER STREET THIS EVENING AT 6.30."

HOLMES HANDED THIS TO PETERSON, WITH THE INSTRUCTION THAT THE ADVERTISEMENT SHOULD APPEAR IN ALL THE LONDON PAPERS THAT EVENING. HE ALSO REQUESTED THAT PETERSON SHOULD BUY A NEW GOOSE ON HIS WAY BACK TO BAKER STREET.

*IT'S A BONNY THING! JUST SEE HOW IT GLINTS AND SPARKLES. OF COURSE IT MAKES CRIMES HAPPEN! EVERY GOOD STONE DOES.*

*DO YOU THINK THIS MAN HENRY BAKER HAS ANYTHING TO DO WITH THE MATTER?*

*I THINK THAT HE IS PERFECTLY INNOCENT. BUT WE SHALL SOON SEE FOR OURSELVES – PROVIDING THAT HE TURNS UP HERE TONIGHT!*

LATER THAT EVENING AT 221B BAKER STREET...

AT 6.30 PRECISELY, A TALL GENTLEMAN ENTERED HOLMES' ROOM AND INTRODUCED HIMSELF AS MR HENRY BAKER. THE GREAT DETECTIVE SOLEMNLY PRESENTED HIM WITH HIS LOST HAT, AND EXPLAINED THAT A REPLACEMENT GOOSE HAD BEEN OBTAINED IN EXCHANGE FOR THE FIRST, WHICH HAD ALREADY BEEN EATEN!

AT THIS, MR HENRY BAKER OFFERED HIS WARMEST THANKS AND GRATITUDE, AND PREPARED TO LEAVE US. AS HE WAS LEAVING A CASUAL INQUIRY FROM HOLMES BROUGHT FORTH THE VALUABLE INFORMATION THAT THE FIRST GOOSE HAD BEEN PROVIDED BY THE LANDLORD OF THE ALPHA INN, WHO HAD ORGANISED A GOOSE CLUB THAT CHRISTMAS FOR HIS CUSTOMERS.

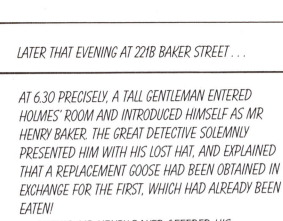

YOUR BEER SHOULD BE EXCELLENT IF IT IS AS GOOD AS YOUR GEESE! I HAVE JUST BEEN SPEAKING TO A MR HENRY BAKER, WHO WAS A MEMBER OF YOUR CHRISTMAS GOOSE CLUB.

AH, YES SIR! THOSE WERE FINE GEESE. I BOUGHT THEM FROM A SALESMAN CALLED BRECKINRIDGE, WHO KEEPS A STALL AT COVENT GARDEN.

FOR SHERLOCK HOLMES, THERE WAS NO TIME LIKE THE PRESENT, AND SO WE SET OFF IMMEDIATELY FOR THE ALPHA INN IN BLOOMSBURY. IT WAS A BITTER NIGHT, SO WE DREW ON OUR HEAVIEST OVERCOATS AND WRAPPED WARM MUFFLERS ROUND OUR THROATS. OUTSIDE, THE STARS WERE SHINING COLDLY IN A CLOUDLESS SKY, AND THE BREATH OF PASSERS-BY LOOKED LIKE PUFFS OF SMOKE. IN A QUARTER OF AN HOUR, WE HAD REACHED THE DOOR OF THE ALPHA INN, AND HAD SOON BEEN SERVED WITH TWO GLASSES OF FOAMING BEER BY THE ROSY-CHEEKED LANDLORD.

AND SO, ARMED WITH THIS INFORMATION, WE CONTINUED OUR JOURNEY TO THE MARKET AT COVENT GARDEN...

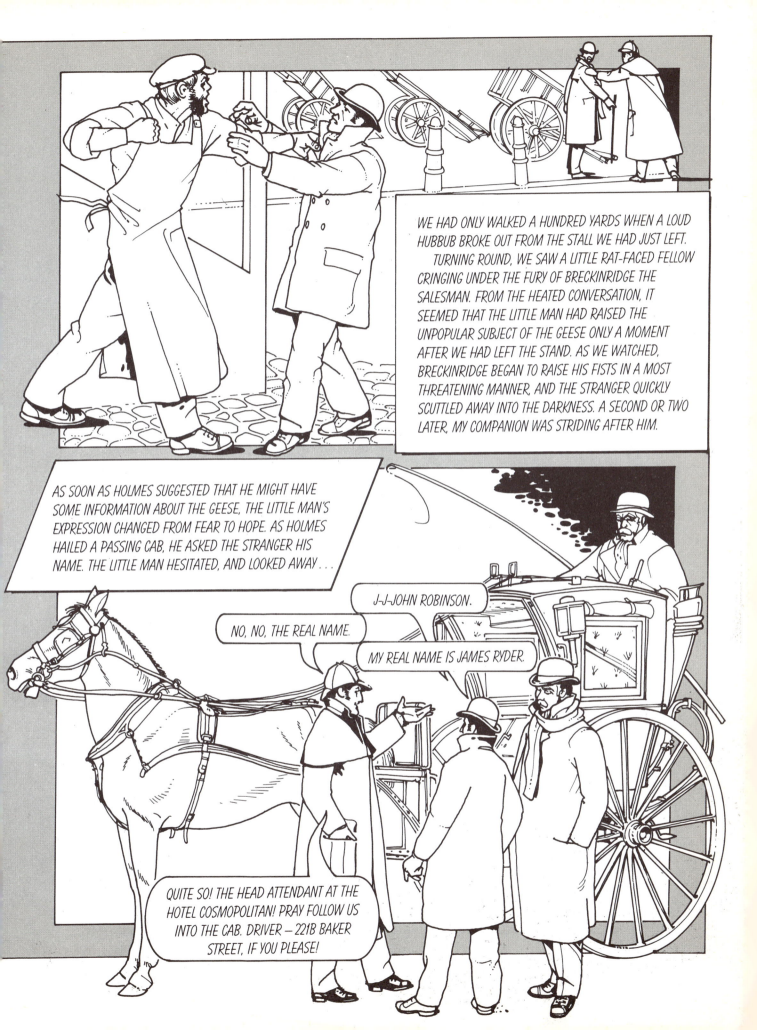

IN HALF AN HOUR, WE WERE BACK IN THE SITTING ROOM AT 221B BAKER STREET...

"I DO NOT WONDER AT YOUR INTEREST IN THE GEESE, MR RYDER — OR RATHER, IN ONE GOOSE IN PARTICULAR! IT LAID SUCH A BRIGHT, BEAUTIFUL EGG! PERHAPS YOU WOULD NOW BE KIND ENOUGH TO EXPLAIN EXACTLY WHAT HAPPENED AFTER YOU STOLE THE CARBUNCLE FROM THE COUNTESS OF MORCA'S ROOM — AFTER THE PLUMBER JOHN HORNER HAD LEFT? COME ON, MAN — THIS IS YOUR ONLY HOPE OF SAVING YOURSELF!"

I WILL TELL YOU, SIR, JUST AS IT HAPPENED. I DID STEAL THE STONE, AS YOU SAY — AND I MADE OUT THAT IT WAS ALL THE FAULT OF JOHN HORNER. I KNEW AT ONCE THAT I HAD TO GET IT AWAY PRETTY QUICK, SO I MADE FOR MY SISTER'S PLACE. SHE RAISES GEESE FOR MARKET ON THE BRIXTON ROAD. IT WAS THERE THAT I HAD MY IDEA FOR HIDING THE STONE. MY SISTER HAD SAID THAT I MIGHT HAVE THE PICK OF HER GEESE FOR CHRISTMAS. I CHOSE ONE, WITH A BAR ON ITS TAIL — AND FORCED THE CARBUNCLE DOWN ITS THROAT! JUST THEN, THE BRUTE JUMPED OUT OF MY ARMS. IT FLAPPED BACK TO THE OTHERS, AND I HAD TO CATCH IT AGAIN. I MANAGED TO KILL IT THIS TIME, AND TOOK IT HOME. WHEN I CUT IT UP LATER, MY HEART TURNED TO WATER. THERE WAS NO SIGN OF THE STONE IN THE BIRD!

# Make a Walkie-Talkie

This is one phone the enemy can't bug!

*All you need are: Two empty tin cans (use the type with lift-off lids); 10 metres strong string; an old candle stump.*

1. Ask an adult to bang a small hole in the base of each can with a nail.

2. Make a small groove in the candle, and run the string along it until it is evenly waxed.

3. Thread the string through the base of the cans, and knot securely in place.

To speak through your walkie-talkie, hold the cans so that the string is pulled taut. For extra secrecy – speak in code!

# Bank Raid

A board game for two players. Before you begin, you will need to trace the counters shown below onto card, and cut them out. Put the money tokens on the matching squares, put the two detectives in DETECTIVE HQ, and the four crooks in their HIDEAWAY. Colour in the board and counters before you begin.

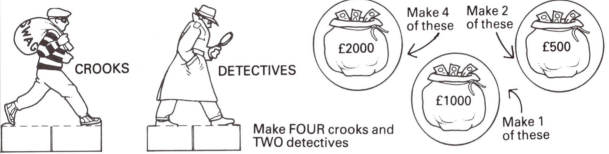

CROOKS

DETECTIVES

Make FOUR crooks and TWO detectives

Make 4 of these £2000

Make 2 of these £500

Make 1 of these £1000

## RULES

1. One player is in charge of the crooks. The other player controls the detectives.

2. Starting with the crooks, each player takes it in turn to move their counters around the board. In any one go, a player must move ONE counter TWO places along (either forwards or backwards).

3. The crooks have to collect the money tokens, by landing on a bank, cafe etc., and get them back to the hideaway without being caught. They must carry the tokens round the board with them as they go. Any crook can pick up more than one token before returning, but they risk losing it all if they are caught by one of the detectives.

4. The detectives chase after the crooks. If a detective lands on a square occupied by a crook, the crook is sent immediately to the Town Jail. Any money they are carrying goes straight to the Detective H.Q.

5. The dark area around the Crooks' Hideaway is the only place on the board where a crook can land on a detective and put him or her out of the game.

6. The game ends EITHER when all the crooks are in jail OR when all the money has been stolen. The player in charge of the detectives scores as follows:
   £500 for each crook in jail PLUS the sum total of the money at H.Q. From this figure, you should subtract:
   £500 for each crook NOT caught, plus the sum total of the money at the Crooks' Hideaway.

7. Keep a note of your score and swop roles.

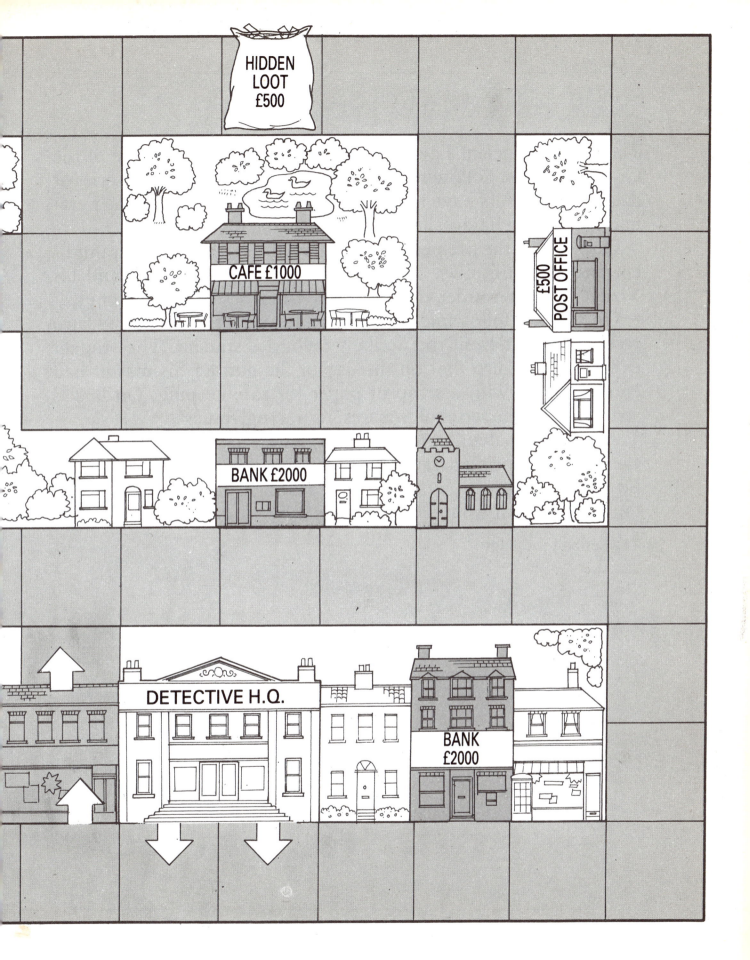

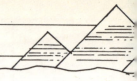

# THE PYRAMID MURDERS

The place is Ancient Egypt. The time is 2800 BC – the age of the Great Pyramids. Following the burial of the last Pharaoh, a series of dastardly murders have taken place near the entrance of the pyramid where the Pharaoh lies buried among all his treasure.

Only two of the five people who knew the secret of the pyramid's entrance are still alive. These are the Pharaoh's widow, and his Vizier. The last murder victim was the Chief Scribe of the Temple.

On the day following the murder, ace detective Ptolemy Cairo received a visit from the Scribe's favourite student. The student explained to Cairo that on the day of the murder his master had entrusted him with a scrap of paper for safe keeping. On it was written a strange series of pictures, or 'hieroglyphics'.

As a keen amateur hieroglyphic expert, Cairo quickly recognized the pictures as being part of a rare Egyptian alphabet. For a moment he was puzzled by the numbers in the message, but it didn't take him long to work out what the Scribe was trying to say.

**The Scribe's message**

WHO KILLED THE CHIEF SCRIBE?
(Remember – things aren't always as they first seem!)

Answer: back page

# S.P.Y.F.I.L.E

According to the James Bond films, top spies are outstandingly handsome, athletic and well-dressed. They jet from one glamorous location to the next, in a series of private helicopters and fast cars. The bad news is that anyone as conspicuous as James Bond would be a dead loss as a spy! Real spies are usually quite ordinary to look at. The work is often boring and routine. Although it is true that

**DISGUISE TIP NO.1:**
COLD WEATHER DISGUISE

**DISGUISE TIP NO.2:**
HOT WEATHER DISGUISE

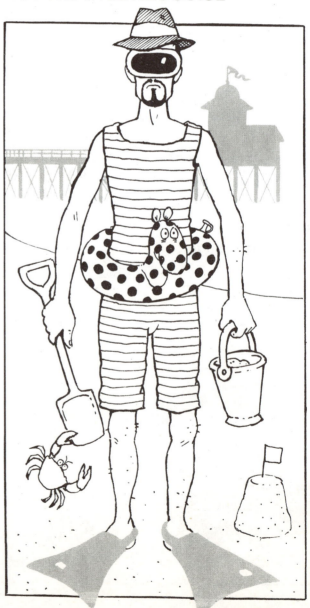

some real-life spies have become famous, we will probably never know about the top ones. They were too good to get caught!

Just like a detective trailing a suspect, a skilful spy will try to blend into his surroundings. You may think that the ideas given below are not entirely serious – but did you know that Lord Baden-Powell, who founded the Scouts movement, once spied very successfully for the British Secret Service in the disguise of a butterfly collector? The sketches he made of butterfly wings had nothing to do with their markings – they showed details of enemy fortifications!

**DISGUISE TIP NO.3:** COUNTRYSIDE DISGUISE

**DISGUISE TIP NO.4:** CITY STREETS DISGUISE

# Foolproof Disguises

Disguise is one of the most important tricks of a spy's trade. Try out some of these ideas, and see how many people you can fool.

Try making yourself look bigger and older. Widen your shoulders by putting a rolled-up towel around your neck – this will also make you look taller. Thicken your waistline with a small cushion or pillow tied on with string. Put on a huge coat, and turn the collar well up.

To look older, dust your skin and hair lightly with talcum powder. Draw on some wrinkles (see opposite). Get some fake spectacles from a joke shop, or wear an old-fashioned pair that have lost their lenses. Walk slowly in a doddery kind of way – or put a pebble in your shoe to make you limp!

## MAKE A BEARD

Hold up a piece of tracing paper in front of your face while looking in the mirror, and use a pencil to mark out a beard shape that fits around your mouth. Cut this out and use it as a stencil to copy the shape onto card. Cut out, cover the card with glue, and stick on strands of brown or yellow wool. When this is dry, make a hole at each end and thread with elastic. Adjust to fit round your head.

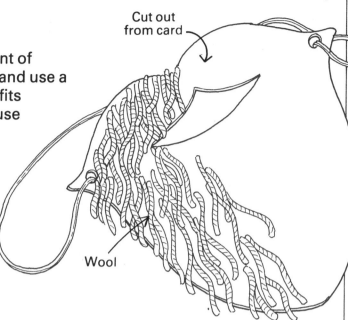

Cut out from card

Wool

### EVERY MASTER OF DISGUISE SHOULD OWN AN EYEBROW PENCIL

With an eyebrow pencil, you can:

★ Draw new eyebrows – blot your own out first with foundation.

★ Give yourself wrinkles – scowl at yourself in the mirror, and use the pencil to draw over the lines that appear on your forehead and around your eyes and mouth.

★ Give yourself a shifty-looking 'five-o'clock-shadow' by drawing stubble marks all over your chin and above your upper lip.

★ Draw a thin moustache.

★ Give yourself a glamorous beauty spot or a mole.

★ Draw a hideous scar onto your cheek.

# A Spy in Your Wardrobe

Make this coat hanger out of stiff card – or ask an adult to mount it on to balsa wood for extra strength. Put the spy to lurk in your wardrobe – or hang it up fully dressed near a window as a decoy to fool the enemy!

1. Trace the spy opposite onto card. Leave plenty of space at either side and below.

2. Make the shoulders wider – lay a wire coat hanger over the spy, as here, and trace around the shape. Cut out.

3. Round off the shoulders like this, and colour in.

Intruders will flee in terror from the spy in your wardrobe!

# Mirror Image

What would you look like in disguise?
Draw yourself in the mirror!

36

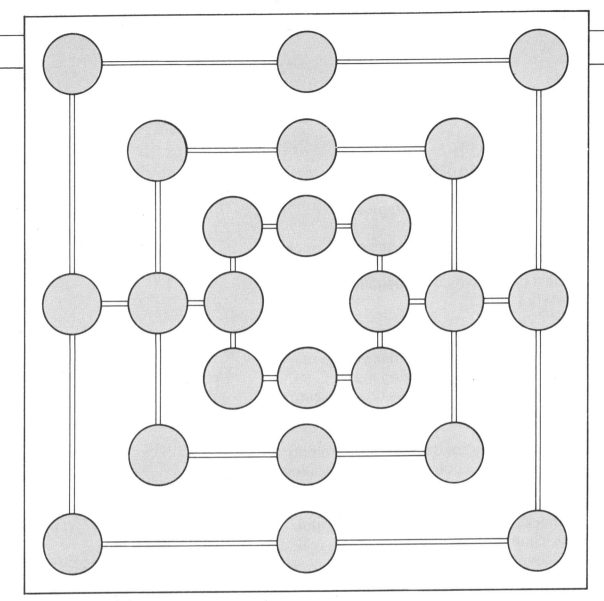

# S.P.Y.T.R.A.C.K.E.R

This is a game for two master spies.

1. Trace the counters on the right. One player should have nine black hats, the other nine white hats.

2. Take it in turns to put a spy counter onto any empty circle on the board. The object is to get three spies in a row along any line.

3. If a player makes a line of three, they may take any one of their opponent's pieces off the board.

4. When all the counters are on the board, take it in turns to move any one of your counters to the next empty circle. Keep trying to make lines of three. You cannot take an opponent's counter if it is already in a line of three – unless these are the only ones they have left.

5. The winner is the player who reduces his or her opponent's spyforce to two counters.

# Keeping Secrets Really Safe

## A BOOK SAFE

*You will need: An old hardback book that nobody wants any more; some stiff card; scissors; a ruler and pencil; glue.*

1. Carefully pull out the pages of the book. (You may find that it's easier to leave the first and last pages, which are usually glued in securely.)

2. Now make a box that is the same width, length and depth as the pages you have taken out. Do this by copying the measurements of the pages onto the card, as shown here.

3. Cut along the solid lines and fold along the dotted ones. Glue the flaps to the sides, to make a box.

4. Check that the box is a good fit for the book. Glue the base of the box to the inside back cover.

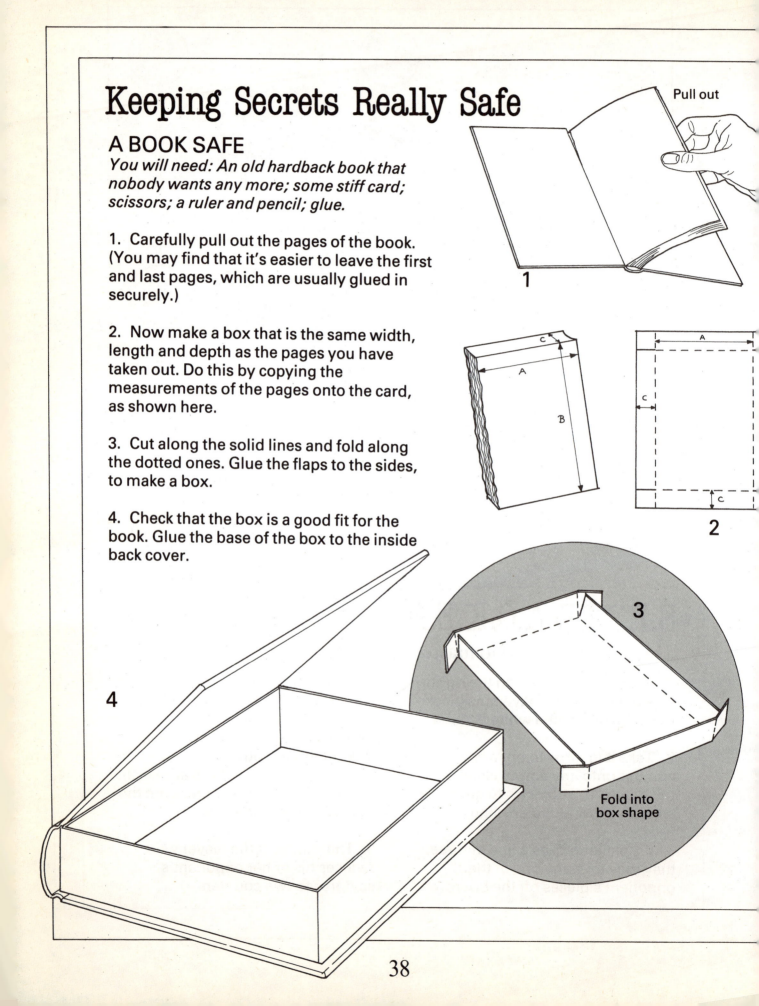

## A STRANGE IDENTITY

If you are working under cover, you may find it useful to pretend to be somebody else. You will be even more convincing if you can casually pull out a wallet full of bits and pieces that back up your false identity. If you are pretending to come from another country, photos taken of you abroad, foreign money, bus tickets and stamps may all help to cover up your silly foreign accent!

## INVISIBLE INK

The juice of oranges, lemons, apples and onions makes very good invisible ink. Write your message on the back of an innocent-looking letter or card – this looks much less suspicious than a blank piece of paper. To read the message, warm it carefully near a central-heating radiator or a light bulb – *never* use a naked flame. The heat will 'cook' the juice, and your secret message will appear.

# SECRET CODES

Spies often have to send urgent messages to their contacts in a way the enemy can't understand. The most difficult codes to crack are the ones you invent yourself — but try these ones first.

### SIMPLE SCRAMBLE

This message (1) is first broken up into two-letter bits (2). Add an extra letter to the end if the number of letters is uneven. Then reverse each pair (3). Add further confusion by closing the letters up again into random chunks. To read the message, all your contact has to do is reverse the process. Your scramble can be as simple or as complicated as you wish.

① BREAK FOR THE BORDER
② BR EA KF OR TH EB OR DE RX
③ RB AE FK RO HT BE RO ED XR
④ RBAEFKR OHTBE ROE D XR

### NOUGHTS AND CROSSES

Copy the four diagrams shown here. To write your message, all you do is draw the pattern that goes with each letter — for example, A is written as ⌐, K is written as ⌐̇ and so on. A variation on this is to write in a key word (it must be a word that does not use the same letter twice) in the first spaces in the diagram. Complete the diagram by filling in all the letters that don't appear in your keyword, in alphabetical order.

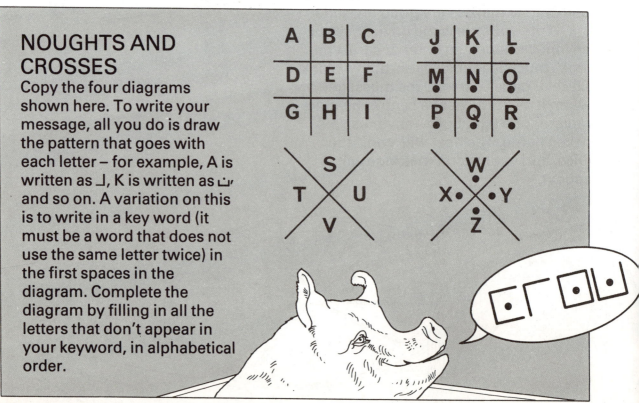

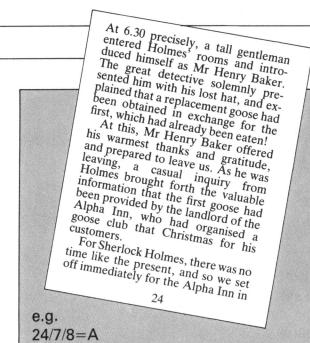

At 6.30 precisely, a tall gentleman entered Holmes' rooms and introduced himself as Mr Henry Baker. The great detective solemnly presented him with his lost hat, and explained that a replacement goose had been obtained in exchange for the first, which had already been eaten!

At this, Mr Henry Baker offered his warmest thanks and gratitude, and prepared to leave us. As he was leaving, a casual inquiry from Holmes brought forth the valuable information that the first goose had been provided by the landlord of the Alpha Inn, who had organised a goose club that Christmas for his customers.

For Sherlock Holmes, there was no time like the present, and so we set off immediately for the Alpha Inn in

24

e.g. 24/7/8=A

## BOOK CODE

You and your contact will need to have the same edition of the same book (it could be one you are using in school).

Each letter is coded in three numbers. The first stands for the page the letter is on. The second number refers to the line, counting down from the top. The third shows how many letters to count, starting from the left.

## SHOPPING LIST

This useful code looks so innocent that you can safely leave it pinned to the kitchen noticeboard!

The secret is in the number at the beginning of each line. Use the number to count along the line, ignoring any abbreviations such as 'oz' or 'lb'.

For example, the letter L could be coded as '2 oz almonds', while '4 lbs flour' refers to the letter U. Can you translate this list? (Answer: back page.)

1 lb sugar
3 lbs butter
2 pkts raisins
1 yoghurt
6 garlic bulbs
4 onions
2 pkts dog biscuits
6 chocolate-chip ice cream

# Make a Code Wheel

Smart spies use code machines. Copy the code wheel shown on these pages — you and your contact will have to make one each.

*For each wheel, you will need: White card; tracing paper; a ruler and pencil; a split pin; scissors.*

1. Trace the two wheels shown opposite onto card. Circles can be quite hard to draw, so ask an older person if they can go over your outlines with a compass before you cut them out. Or, you could ask someone to photocopy the page, and stick it onto card.

2. Cut out the circles, and link them in the middle with the split pin, as shown.

3. To use the wheel, you will first have to agree a KEY NUMBER with your contact. Write out your message, ignoring any word breaks, and then keep writing the key number over the top. For example, let's say you choose 1949 as your key number, and the message is CAFE MOZART, EIGHT O'CLOCK:

1 9 4 9 1 9 4 9 1 9
C A F E M O Z A R T
4 9 1 9 4 9 1 9 4 9 1
E I G H T O C L O C K

4. Turn the smaller wheel until the arrow is pointing to the first number in your key (number 1). Now look for the first letter in your message (letter C). Opposite it on the larger wheel you should find the letter Y. This becomes the first letter in your code. To find the

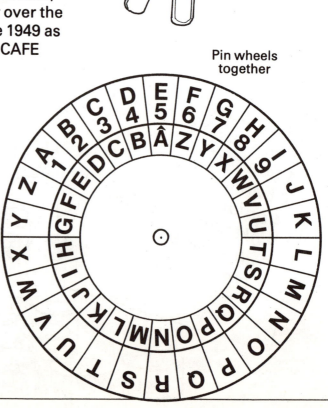

Pin wheels together

second letter, turn the arrow to 9, and see what lines up with the letter A. You should find that it lines up with I. The eventual code should read like this:

Y I Y E O U E I J P

Z A U B K U Y X P G Q

To decode the message, your contact simply reverses the process!

# The Lost Codebook

The spy is a stranger in town. Every morning, a coded message arrives at his hotel room, giving him the name of the rendezvous point where he must meet his contact.

It is now Friday, and the spy has a problem. During the night his room was raided and his codebook stolen. Miserably, the spy stares at his coded message, wondering how he is to decipher it. Suddenly he remembers that he has kept a note of the messages he received on the previous three days. He knows that on Tuesday he met his contact at a church. On Wednesday, they met at an inn. On Thursday they met in a cinema foyer.

Can you help the spy work out where he should be going today? (Answer: back page.)

# THE TOTALLY SECRET P.A.R.T.Y.

Scotland Yard or MI5 may not call this week – but you can still practise your cloak-and-dagger skills by throwing a top secret party.

## THE INVITATION
This, of course, should be written in a code that is known only to your guests. Why not include a special assignment for each one? For example, you could secretly instruct one friend to tail another to the party. Then, without either of the first two knowing, you could tell another friend to follow the one who is tailing the first friend!

## SECRET THINGS TO DO
Spies and detectives have to be observant. How do your friends shape up? As they arrive, hand them a list of objects that are cleverly hidden in the room, and tell them that they should be able to find them without touching anything. The objects could be anything from a red ball hidden in a bowl of red apples, to an object shown in a painting on the wall.

## MURDER IN THE DARK

The best secret games are played in the dark. For this game, make as many slips of paper as there are guests. Write D (for detective) on one, M (for murderer) on another, and leave the rest blank. Shuffle the pieces and ask each guest to choose one without looking. Apart from the detective, who immediately goes to stand by the light switch, no-one tells anyone which slip they have drawn. The detective now turns off the lights.

Stealthily, the player who has drawn M moves towards the shadowy shape of a victim. Once the victim feels the murderer's tap on their shoulder, he or she utters a gruesome scream before dropping to the floor. The detective counts to three, and turns on the lights.

The detective now questions each player in turn about their movements. Only the murderer is allowed to lie. (The murderer is also the only one who should move once the victim has screamed.) If the detective's first guess is correct, the players draw again. If the guess is wrong, the first victim is carried out, the lights are turned off – and the killer strikes yet again!

# It's Time to Come up with Some Answers!

## Page 28

First of all, Cairo uses the rare hieroglyphic alphabet to translate the Scribe's message. This reads as follows:

PHARAOH'S WIFE IN DANGER. VIZIER PLANS TO STEAL TREASURE FROM PYRAMID. DO NOT TRUST HIM. TELL HER NOT TO GIVE VIZIER INFORMATION. GIVE CAIRO THIS MESSAGE IF I DIE THIS NIGHT.

However, Cairo's detective training tells him that those numbers are there for a purpose. He uses them to count along the symbols in the message. For example, the first number is 1 and the first symbol translates as PHARAOH. The second number is 2, and the second symbol means WIFE. The third number is 7, and the third symbol means PLANS. Put together, the entire message reads:

PHARAOH'S WIFE PLANS TO STEAL TREASURE FROM PYRAMID. DO NOT TRUST HER. GIVE CAIRO THIS MESSAGE IF I DIE THIS NIGHT.

A very different story from the first translation!

## Page 41

The Shopping List Code translates as:

STAY COOL

## Page 44

Looking at the coded message for Thursday, the spy finds that the third and fifth symbols are the same. The only cinemas in town are the Ritzy, the Odeon and the Plaza, and of these only the Plaza has the same third and fifth letters. The Spy can therefore work out the symbols for P, L, A and Z, and use this information to work out that the code for Tuesday translates as ST MARK and the code for Wednesday translates as THE PIG AND SCEPTRE.

By this time, he has enough letters to work out that he must meet his contact at the Post Office.